YVOR WINTERS : *COLLECTED POEMS*

COLLECTED POEMS

by YVOR WINTERS

ALAN SWALLOW

To Professor and Mrs. Richard Foster Jones
with admiration and affection

ACKNOWLEDGMENTS

The first four poems in this volume are from *The Immobile Wind,* published by Monroe Wheeler, Evanston, Ill., 1921 (copyright by Monroe Wheeler, 1921).

Of the next five, two are from *The Magpie's Shadow,* Chicago (copyright by Musterbookhouse, 1922); one is from *The Bare Hills,* The Four Seas Company, Boston (copyright by The Four Seas Company, 1927); and two, though equally early, were first printed in my *Poems,* The Gyroscope Press (copyright by Yvor Winters, 1940).

Of the remaining poems preceding the translations, all save two are from *The Bare Hills.* The Goatherds, Song of the Trees, and the poems which follow the translations and precede The Slow Pacific Swell, are from *The Proof* (copyright by Coward McCann, Inc., 1930).

The next poems, preceding Anacreontic, are from *The Journey,* The Dragon Press, Ithaca, N. Y. (copyright by Yvor Winters, 1931).

From Anacreontic to Chiron, inclusive, and one poem excepted, the poems come from *Before Disaster,* Tryon Pamphlets, Tryon, N. C. (copyright by Yvor Winters, 1934).

Six of the remaining poems have appeared in *Twelve Poets of the Pacific,* an anthology edited by myself and published by New Directions (copyright by New Directions, 1937).

All of the poems thus far mentioned appeared in my *Poems,* The Gyroscope Press, already mentioned.

Five of the poems here included first appeared in book form in *The Giant Weapon,* New Directions (copyright by New Directions, 1943).

Three of the poems here included have appeared in

Three Poems, a pamphlet issued by The Cummington Press (copyright by Yvor Winters, 1950).

Acknowledgment is due likewise to the following periodicals, which range from annuals to dailies: The American Caravan, Avenue, Contact, The Dial, The Forge, The Hound and Horn, The Hudson Review, The Magazine, The Miscellany, Modern Verse, The Nation, New Mexico Quarterly Review, The New Republic, The New York Times, New Verse, "1924," Pagany, Poetry (Chicago), Prairie, The Rocking Horse, Secession, Smoke, The Southern Review, and This Quarter.

New Directions claims the right to collect all anthology fees for poems appearing in *The Giant Weapon* and to retain one third of these fees. The poems in question are the following: *By the Road to the Air-Base, The Cremation, Before Disaster, To My Infant Daughter, The Marriage, Dedication for a Book of Criticism, Sonnet to the Moon, To Edwin V. McKenzie, To David Lamson, Heracles, Orpheus, The Manzanita, Elegy on a Young Airedale Bitch, A Spring Serpent, An October Nocturne, A Winter Evening, To a Military Rifle, For the Opening of the William Dinsmore Briggs Room, John Day, Frontiersman, A Summer Commentary, John Sutter, On Teaching the Young, Sir Gawaine and the Green Knight, Chiron, On Rereading a Passage from John Muir, An Elegy for the U.S.N. Dirigible, "Macon," Time and the Garden, Much in Little, A Prayer for My Son, Midas, On a Portrait of a Scholar of the Italian Renaissance, Summer Noon: 1941, A Testament.* Any anthologist who may wish to use one of the poems listed in this paragraph must obtain permission from New Directions; any anthologist wishing to use any other poem herein published must obtain permission from Alan Swallow.

CONTENTS

A SONG OF ADVENT

On the desert, between pale mountains, our cries:
Far whispers creeping through an ancient shell.

SONG

I could tell
Of silence where
One ran before
Himself and fell
Into silence
Yet more fair.

Sweeter than rough hair
On earth there is none:
Rough as the wind
And brown as the sun!

I toss high my short arms,
Brown as the sun!
I creep on the mountains
And never am done!

Sharp-hoofed, hard-eyed,
Trample on the sun!
Sharp ears, stiff as wind,
Point the way to run!

Who on the brown earth
Knows himself one?
Life is in lichens
That sleep as they run.

ALONE

I, one who never speaks,
Listened days in summer trees,
Each day a rustling leaf!
Then, in time, my unbelief
Grew like my running:
My own eyes did not exist!
When I struck I never missed!
Noon, felt and far away,
My brain is a thousand bees.

THE LIE

I paved a sky
  With days.
I crept beyond the Lie.
  This phrase,
Yet more profound,
  Grew where
I was not. I
  Was there.

NOON

Did you move, in the sun?

THE SHADOW'S SONG

I am beside you, now.

THE ASPEN'S SONG

The summer holds me here.

GOD OF ROADS

I, peregrine of noon.

SLEEP

O living pine, be still!

Junipers,
Steely shadows,
Floating the jay.
A man,

Heavy and iron-black,
Alone in sun,
Threading the grass.
The cold,

Coming again
As Spring
Came up the valley,
But to stay

Rooted deep in the land.
The stone-pierced shadows
Trod by the bird
For day on day.

A pale horse,
Mane of flowery dust,
Runs too far for a sound
To cross the river.

Afternoon,
Swept by far hooves
That gleam
Like slow fruit
Falling
In the haze
Of pondered vision.

It is nothing.
Afternoon
Beyond a child's thought,
Where a falling stone
Would raise pale earth,
A fern ascending.

The harvest falls
Throughout the valleys
With a sound
Of fire in leaves.

The harsh trees,
Heavy with light,
Beneath the flame, and aging,
Have risen high and higher.

Apricots,
The clustered
Fur of bees
Above the gray rocks of the uplands.

The hunter deep in summer.
Grass laid low by what comes,
Feet or air—
But motion, aging.

The trees are
the rayed pillars
of the sun where
small boys gather
seashells in the desert;
goats move here and there;
the small boys
shriek amid white rocks,
run at the river;
and the sky has
risen in red dust
and stricken
villages with distance
till the brown feet quiver
on the rock like
fallen eyelids and the
goat's hoof, tiny,
jet, is like a twig about
to burst in flame.

       And then
the motion once again like
tiny blossoms
far away beside the river
and the cries of
small boys like the
cries of birds at dawn.

Belief is blind! Bees scream!
Gongs! Thronged with light!

       And I take
into light, hold light,
in light I live, I,
pooled and broken here,
to watch, to wake above you.

       Sun,
no seeming, but savage
simplicity, breaks running
for an aeon, stops, shuddering, here.

THE COLD

Frigidity the hesitant
uncurls its tentacles
into a furry sun.
The ice expands
into an insecurity
that should appal
yet I remain
astray in this
oblivion, this
inert labyrinth
of sentences that
dare not end. It
is high noon and
all is the more quiet
where I trace
the courses of the Crab
and Scorpion, the Bull,
the Hunter, and the Bear—
with front of steel
they cut an aperture
so clear across the
cold that it cannot
be seen: there is no
smoky breath, no
breath at all.

Earth darkens and is beaded
with a sweat of bushes and
the bear comes forth;
the mind, stored with
magnificence, proceeds into
the mystery of time, now
certain of its choice of
passion, but uncertain of the
passion's end.

When
Plato temporizes on the nature
of the plumage of the soul the
wind hums in the feathers as
across a cord impeccable in
tautness but of no mind:

Time,
the sine-pondere, most
imperturbable of elements,
assumes its own proportions
silently, of its own properties—
an excellence at which one
sighs.

Adventurer in
living fact, the poet
mounts into the spring,
upon his tongue the taste of
air becoming body: is
embedded in this crystalline
precipitate of time.

NOCTURNE

Moonlight on stubbleshining hills
whirls down upon me finer than geometry
and at my very
face it blurs and softens like a dream

In leafblack houses
linen smooth with sleep
and folded by cold life itself for limbs so definite

their passion is
persistent like a pane of glass

about their feet the clustered
birds are sleeping
heavy with incessant life

The dogs swim close to earth

A kildee rises
dazed and rolled amid the sudden blur of sleep
above the dayglare of the fields
goes screaming
off toward darker hills

SONG

Where I walk out
to meet you on the
cloth of burning
fields

the goldfinches
leap up about my
feet like angry
dandelions

quiver like a
heartbeat in the
air and are
no more

APRIL

The little goat
crops
new grass lying down
leaps up eight inches
into air and
lands on four feet.
Not a tremor—
solid in the
spring and serious
he walks away.

THE COLD ROOM

The dream
stands
in the night
above unpainted
floor and chair.

The dog is
dead asleep
and
will not move
for god or fire.

And from the
ceiling
darkness bends
a heavy flame.

THE BARNYARD

The wind appears
and disappears
like breath on a mirror
and between the hills
is only cold
that lies
beneath the stones
and in the grass.
The sleeping dog
becomes a
knot of twinging turf.
It was the
spring that left
this rubbish
and these scavengers
for ice to kill—
this old man
wrinkled in
the fear of Hell, the
child that staggers
straight into
the clotting cold
with short fierce cries.

To be my own Messiah to the
burning end. Can one endure the
acrid, steeping darkness of
the brain, which glitters and is
dissipated? Night. The night is
winter and a dull man bending,
muttering above a freezing pipe;
and I, bent heavily on books; the
mountain iron in my sleep and
ringing; but the pipe has frozen, haired with
unseen veins, and cold is on the eyelids: who can
remedy this vision?

                        I have walked upon
the streets between the trees that
grew unleaved from asphalt in a night of
sweating winter in distracted silence.

                        I have
walked among the tombs—the rushing of the air
in the rich pines above my head is that which
ceaseth not nor stirreth whence it is:
in this the sound of wind is like a flame.

It was the dumb decision of the
madness of my youth that left me with
this cold eye for the fact; that keeps me
quiet, walking toward a
stinging end: I am alone,
and, like the alligator cleaving timeless mud,
among the blessed who have Latin names.

THE LADY'S FAREWELL
from the 13th century Galician

Awake, my love, who sleep into the dawn!
The birds of all the world cried and are gone.
I go away in joy.

Awake, my love, who sleep so late at dawn!
It was our love the small birds dwelt upon.
I go away in joy.

The birds of all the world spoke of our love,
Of my love and of yours cried out above.
I go away in joy.

The birds of all the world sang loud at day.
It was my love and yours, I heard them say.
I go away in joy.

It was my love and yours that made their song.
You cut the branches where they clung so long.
I go away in joy.

It was my love and yours that made their cry—
You cut the branches where they used to fly.
I go away in joy.

You cut the branches where they used to sing,
And where they came to drink you dried the spring.
I go away in joy.

You cut the branches where they used to stay,
And dried the waters where they came to play.
I go away in joy.

—Nuño Fernández Torneol

COSSANTE

from the 13th century Galician

Tell me, daughter, my pretty daughter,
Why you waited by the cold water.
   —It was love, alas!

Tell me, daughter, my lovely daughter,
Why you waited by the cold water.
   —It was love, alas!

I waited, mother, by the cold fountain
While the deer came down the mountain.
   —It was love, alas!

I waited by the cold river, mother,
To see the deer, and not for any other.
   —It was love, alas!

You lie, daughter, you lie for your lover,
I never saw deer come down from cover.
   —It was love, alas!

You lie, daughter, for your lover by the fountain,
I never saw deer going up to the mountain.
   —It was love, alas!

       —Pero Meogo

POEM
from the Spanish
of the 16th century

Nothing move thee;
Nothing terrify thee;
Everything passes;
God never changes.
Patience be all to thee.
Who trusts in God, he
Never shall be needy.
God alone suffices.

—Saint Theresa

DEATH'S WARNINGS
from the 17th century Spanish

I looked upon the old walls of my land—
Once they were strong, and now they fall away.
Tired with the march of age, they may not stay—
Their strength has vanished, and they scarcely stand.
    I went out to the fields, and from the sand
The sun drank up the brooks that broke to play
And drank the crying flocks that stole the day
From off the mountain with their shadowy band.

    I went into my house, and there I found
The rotted leavings of an ancient race:
I found my staff more twisted and less sound,
    I felt my sword that crumbled at the breath
Of age, and saw no thing in all the place
That did not seem an harbinger of death.

—Francisco de Quevedo y Villegas

Agëd orchards, gently flowing
Waters of the clearest fountains,
Thin air of the higher mountains,
Little valleys always shining
With white houses and black towers
And the sea forever creeping,
Where the spirit broods in quiet,
Blessëd sweat upon the forehead—
This it is inspires my hours,
And with these Cantabria keeps me.
Should I vanish, let them seek me
From Higuer to Finisterre.

—Antonio de Trueba

ROME
from the 16th century French

You, who behold in wonder Rome and all
Her former passion, menacing the gods,
These ancient palaces and baths, the sods
Of seven hills, and temple, arch, and wall,
    Consider, in the ruins of her fall,
That which destroying Time has gnawed away—
What workmen built with labor day by day
Only a few worn fragments now recall.

Then look again and see where, endlessly
Treading upon her own antiquity,
Rome has rebuilt herself with works as just:
    There you may see the demon of the land
Forcing himself again with fatal hand
To raise the city from this ruined dust.

—Joachim du Bellay

REFLECTIONS
from the 17th century French

I

Why rejoice in beauty? What
In all the world is half so vain?
    Nay, there is naught
    Gives so much pain.
I know that over hearts her rule is sore,
    While one is beautiful that she
May have of passion and of lovers store:
    But that has little time to be
    And a long time to be no more.

II

Pathetic plaything of a witless chance,
    Victim of evils and of laws,
    Man, who in whatever cause,
    Must suffer life's impertinence,
      Still, after all that's past,
Whence comes it that you fear the power of death?
Coward! regard it with unhurried breath,
    And know this outrage for the last.

—Madame des Houlières

THE SKELETON LABORER

Written to the flayed and fleshless
figures on an anatomical chart
from the 19th century French

Out of the earth at which you spade,
Funereal laborers, tired and done,
Out of your straining naked bone,
Out of your muscles bare and frayed,

Tell me, what harvest do you win?
Slaves snatched from the charnel ground,
Who is the farmer drives this round
To fill his barn? And what your sin?

You, the terrible sign we're shown
Of our destiny's greater dearth,
Wish you to say that in the earth
The promised sleep is never known?

That the end has betrayed us here,
That even death himself has lied?
That though eternity betide,
Alas! we have again to fear

That in some unknown land we'll meet
A knotted earth that needs be flayed—
To drive again the heavy spade
Beneath our bleeding naked feet?

                              —Charles Baudelaire

GREEN
from the 19th century French

Here you have fruits and flowers and boughs with leaves,
And then my heart, which beats for you alone—
May your white hands not tear it—humble sheaves!
May they seem sweet to you when they are shown!

I come again all covered with the dew
That morning wind has frozen on my brow.
Suffer my weariness, at rest near you,
To dream of quiet that I come to now.

Upon this young breast, let my dull head fall,
Ringing with your last kisses; this, and, best,
Let it grow quiet there from storm and all
In a brief sleep, since you too are at rest.

—Paul Verlaine

A SIGH
from the 19th century French

Calm sister, toward your quiet brow where dreams
Roan autumn, toward the questing heaven of
Your eye, my soul mounts steadily; it seems
A jet of water sighing faithfully
Toward heaven in some worn garden; and, above,
October's blue is tender, pale, and pure,
And looks into the fountain with its sure
And infinite languor; in tawn agony
The leaves go with the wind and mark a dun
Hard furrow near a long cold line of sun.

—Stéphane Mallarmé

MARINE
from the 19th century French

The chariots of silver and copper,
The prows of steel and of silver,
Beat foam,
Tear up the blackberry stems.

Land-currents,
The immense paths of the reflux,
File in a circle to eastward,
Toward the columns of the forest,
Towards the piles of the jetty,
The angle of which is hit by the whirlwinds of light.

—Arthur Rimbaud

THE MORALISTS

You would extend the mind beyond the act,
Furious, bending, suffering in thin
And unpoetic dicta; you have been
Forced by hypothesis to fiercer fact.
As metal singing hard, with firmness racked,
You formulate our passion; and behind
In some harsh moment nowise of the mind
Lie the old meanings your advance has packed.

No man can hold existence in the head.
I, too, have known the anguish of the right
Amid this net of mathematic dearth,
And the brain throbbing like a ship at night:
Have faced with old unmitigated dread
The hard familiar wrinkles of the earth.

Death. Nothing is simpler. One is dead.
The set face now will fade out; the bare fact,
Related movement, regular, intact,
Is reabsorbed, the clay is on the bed.
The soul is mortal, nothing: the dim head
On the dim pillow, less. But thought clings flat
To this, since it can never follow that
Where no precision of the mind is bred.

Nothing to think of between you and All!
Screaming processionals of infinite
Logic are grinding down receding cold!
O fool! Madness again! Turn not, for it
Lurks in each paintless cranny, and you sprawl
Blurring a definition. Quick! you are old.

Amid the walls' insensate white, some crime
Is redefined above the sunken mass
Of crumbled years; logic reclaims the crass,
Frees from historic dross the invidious mime.
Your fingers spin the pages into Time;
And in between, moments of darkness pass
Like undiscovered instants in the glass,
Amid the image, where the demons climb.

Climb and regard and mean, yet not emerge.
And in the godless thin electric glare
I watch your face spun momently along
Till the dark moments close and wrinkles verge
On the definitive and final stare:
And that hard book will now contain this wrong.

THE INVADERS

They have won out at last and laid us bare,
The demons of the meaning of the dead,
Stripped us with wheel and flame. Oh, where they tread,
Dissolves our heritage of earth and air!
Till as a locomotive plunges through
Distance that has no meaning and no bound
Thundering some interminable sound
To inward metal where its motion grew—

Grew and contracted down through infinite
And sub-atomic roar of Time on Time
Toward meaning that its changing cannot find;
So, stripped of color of an earth, and lit
With motion only of some inner rime,
The naked passion of the human mind.

TO EMILY DICKINSON

Dear Emily, my tears would burn your page,
But for the fire-dry line that makes them burn—
Burning my eyes, my fingers, while I turn
Singly the words that crease my heart with age.
If I could make some tortured pilgrimage
Through words or Time or the blank pain of Doom
And kneel before you as you found your tomb,
Then I might rise to face my heritage.

Yours was an empty upland solitude
Bleached to the powder of a dying name;
The mind, lost in a word's lost certitude
That faded as the fading footsteps came
To trace an epilogue to words grown odd
In that hard argument which led to God.

Through autumn evening, water whirls thin blue,
From iron to iron pail—old, lined, and pure;
Beneath, the iron is indistinct, secure
In revery that cannot reach to you.
Water it was that always lay between
The mind of man and that harsh wall of thorn,
Of stone impenetrable, where the horn
Hung like the key to what it all might mean.

My goats step guardedly, with delicate
Hard flanks and forest hair, unchanged and firm,
A strong tradition that has not grown old.
Peace to the lips that bend in intricate
Old motions, that flinch not before their term!
Peace to the heart that can accept this cold!

APOLLO AND DAPHNE

Deep in the leafy fierceness of the wood,
Sunlight, the cellular and creeping pyre,
Increased more slowly than aetherial fire:
But it increased and touched her where she stood.
The god had seized her, but the powers of good
Struck deep into her veins; with rending flesh
She fled all ways into the grasses' mesh
And burned more quickly than the sunlight could.

And all her heart broke stiff in leafy flame
That neither rose nor fell, but stood aghast;
And she, rooted in Time's slow agony,
Stirred dully, hard-edged laurel, in the past;
And, like a cloud of silence or a name,
The god withdrew into Eternity.

Beyond the steady rock the steady sea,
In movement more immovable than station,
Gathers and washes and is gone. It comes,
A slow obscure metonymy of motion,
Crumbling the inner barriers of the brain.
But the crossed rock braces the hills and makes
A steady quiet of the steady music,
Massive with peace.

             And listen, now:
The foam receding down the sand silvers
Between the grains, thin, pure as virgin words,
Lending a sheen to Nothing, whispering.

THE EMPTY HILLS
Flintridge, Pasadena

The grandeur of deep afternoons,
The pomp of haze on marble hills,
Where every white-walled villa swoons
Through violence that heat fulfills,

Pass tirelessly and more alone
Than kings that time has laid aside.
Safe on their massive sea of stone
The empty tufted gardens ride.

Here is no music, where the air
Drives slowly through the airy leaves.
Meaning is aimless motion where
The sinking hummingbird conceives.

No book nor picture has inlaid
This life with darkened gold, but here
Men passionless and dumb invade
A quiet that entrances fear.

Here where I watch the dew
That gathers by the door,
Here where the time is true
   And on the floor
My shadow stirs no more,

The slow night burns away.
Nay, neither I nor Time
Can manage quite to stay—
   We seek a clime
Bound in a moment's chime.

Men are like blades of grass
Beneath a winter sky,
The constellations pass,
   The air is dry
From star to living eye.

Hence unto God, unsought,
My anguish sets. Oh, vain
The heart that hates! Oh, naught
   So drenched in pain!
Grief will not turn again.

MOONRISE

The slow moon draws
The shadows through the leaves.
The change it weaves
Eludes design or pause.

And here we wait
In moon a little space,
And face to face
We know the hour grows late.

We turn from sleep
And hold our breath a while,
As mile on mile
The terror drifts more deep.

So we must part
In ruin utterly—
Reality
Invades the crumbling heart.

We scarce shall weep
For what no change retrieves.
The moon and leaves
Shift here and there toward sleep.

The green has suddenly
Divided to pure flame,
Leaf-tongued from tree to tree.
Yea, where we stood it came.

This change may have no name.
Yet it was like a word;
Spoken and none to blame,
Alive where shadow stirred.

So was the instant blurred.
But as we waited there,
The slow cry of a bird
Built up a scheme of air.

The vision of despair
Starts at the moment's bound,
Seethes from the vibrant air
With slow autumnal sound

Into the burning ground.

When men are laid away,
Revolving seasons bring
New love, corrupting clay
And hearts dissevering.

Hearts that were once so fast,
Sickened with living blood,
Will rot to change at last.
The dead have hardihood.

Death is Eternity,
And all who come there stay.
For choice, now certainty.
No moment breaks away.

Amid this wilderness,
Dazed in a swarm of hours,—
Birds tangled numberless!—
Archaic Summer towers.

The dead are left alone—
Theirs the intenser cost.
You followed to a stone,
And there the trail was lost.

THE LAST VISIT
For Henry Ahnefeldt, 1862-1929

The drift of leaves grows deep, the grass
Is longer everywhere I pass.
And listen! where the wind is heard,
The surface of the garden's blurred—
It is the passing wilderness.
The garden will be something less
When others win it back from change.
We shall not know it then; a strange
Presence will be musing there.
Ruin has touched familiar air,
And we depart. Where you should be,
I sought a final memory.

Now autumn's end draws down
Hard twilight by the door;
The wash of rain will drown
Our evening words no more.

Words we have had in store.
But men must move apart
Though what has gone before
Have changed the living heart.

Music and strength of art
Beneath long winter rain
Have played the living part,
With the firm mind for gain.

Nor is the mind in vain.

Far out of sight forever stands the sea,
Bounding the land with pale tranquillity.
When a small child, I watched it from a hill
At thirty miles or more. The vision still
Lies in the eye, soft blue and far away:
The rain has washed the dust from April day;
Paint-brush and lupine lie against the ground;
The wind above the hill-top has the sound
Of distant water in unbroken sky;
Dark and precise the little steamers ply—
Firm in direction they seem not to stir.
That is illusion. The artificer
Of quiet, distance holds me in a vise
And holds the ocean steady to my eyes.

Once when I rounded Flattery, the sea
Hove its loose weight like sand to tangle me
Upon the washing deck, to crush the hull;
Subsiding, dragged flesh at the bone. The skull
Felt the retreating wash of dreaming hair.
Half drenched in dissolution, I lay bare.
I scarcely pulled myself erect; I came
Back slowly, slowly knew myself the same.
That was the ocean. From the ship we saw
Gray whales for miles: the long sweep of the jaw,
The blunt head plunging clean above the wave.
And one rose in a tent of sea and gave
A darkening shudder; water fell away;
The whale stood shining, and then sank in spray.

A landsman, I. The sea is but a sound.
I would be near it on a sandy mound,
And hear the steady rushing of the deep
While I lay stinging in the sand with sleep.
I have lived inland long. The land is numb.
It stands beneath the feet, and one may come
Walking securely, till the sea extends
Its limber margin, and precision ends.
By night a chaos of commingling power,
The whole Pacific hovers hour by hour.
The slow Pacific swell stirs on the sand,
Sleeping to sink away, withdrawing land,
Heaving and wrinkled in the moon, and blind;
Or gathers seaward, ebbing out of mind.

THE MARRIAGE

Incarnate for our marriage you appeared,
Flesh living in the spirit and endeared
By minor graces and slow sensual change.
Through every nerve we made our spirits range.
We fed our minds on every mortal thing:
The lacy fronds of carrots in the spring,
Their flesh sweet on the tongue, the salty wine
From bitter grapes, which gathered through the vine
The mineral drouth of autumn concentrate,
Wild spring in dream escaping, the debate
Of flesh and spirit on those vernal nights,
Its resolution in naive delights,
The young kids bleating softly in the rain—
All this to pass, not to return again.
And when I found your flesh did not resist,
It was the living spirit that I kissed,
It was the spirit's change in which I lay:
Thus, mind in mind we waited for the day.
When flesh shall fall away, and, falling, stand
Wrinkling with shadow over face and hand,
Still I shall meet you on the verge of dust
And know you as a faithful vestige must.
And, in commemoration of our lust,
May our heirs seal us in a single urn,
A single spirit never to return.

ON A VIEW OF PASADENA
FROM THE HILLS

From the high terrace porch I watch the dawn.
No light appears, though dark has mostly gone,
Sunk from the cold and monstrous stone. The hills
Lie naked but not light. The darkness spills
Down the remoter gulleys; pooled, will stay
Too low to melt, not yet alive with day.
Below the windows, the lawn, matted deep
Under its close-cropped tips with dewy sleep,
Gives off a faint hush, all its plushy swarm
Alive with coolness reaching to be warm.
Gray windows at my back, the massy frame
Dull with the blackness that has not a name;
But down below, the garden is still young,
Of five years' growth, perhaps, and terrace-hung,
Drop by slow drop of seeping concrete walls.
Such are the bastions of our pastorals!

Here are no palms! They once lined country ways,
Where old white houses glared down dusty days,
With small round towers, blunt-headed through small trees.
Those towers are now the hiving place of bees.
The palms were coarse; their leaves hung thick with dust;
The roads were muffled deep. But now deep rust
Has fastened on the wheels that labored then.
Peace to all such, and to all sleeping men!
I lived my childhood there, a passive dream
In the expanse of that recessive scheme.

Slow air, slow fire! O deep delay of Time!
That summer crater smoked like slaking lime,
The hills so dry, so dense the underbrush,
That where I pushed my way the giant hush
Was changed to soft explosion as the sage
Broke down to powdered ash, the sift of age,
And fell along my path, a shadowy rift.

On these rocks now no burning ashes drift;
Mowed lawn has crept along the granite bench;
The yellow blossoms of acacia drench
The dawn with pollen; and, with waxen green,
The long leaves of the eucalypti screen
The closer hills from view—lithe, tall, and fine,
And nobly clad with youth, they bend and shine.
The small dark pool, jutting with living rock,
Trembles at every atmospheric shock,
Blurred to its depth with the cold living ooze.
From cloudy caves, heavy with summer dews,
The shyest and most tremulous beings stir,
The pulsing of their fins a lucent blur,
That, like illusion, glances off the view.
The pulsing mouths, like metronomes, are true.

This is my father's house, no homestead here
That I shall live in, but a shining sphere
Of glass and glassy moments, frail surprise,
My father's phantasy of Paradise;
Which melts upon his death, which he attained
With loss of heart for every step he gained.
Too firmly gentle to displace the great,
He crystallized this vision somewhat late;

Forbidden now to climb the garden stair,
He views the terrace from a window chair.
His friends, hard shaken by some twenty years,
Tremble with palsy and with senile fears,
In their late middle age gone cold and gray.
Fine men, now broken. That the vision stay,
They spend astutely their depleted breath,
With tired ironic faces wait for death.

Below the garden the hills fold away.
Deep in the valley, a mist fine as spray,
Ready to shatter into spinning light,
Conceals the city at the edge of night.
The city, on the tremendous valley floor,
Draws its dream deeper for an instant more,
Superb on solid loam, and breathing deep,
Poised for a moment at the edge of sleep.

Cement roads mark the hills, wide, bending free
Of cliff and headland. Dropping toward the sea,
Through suburb after suburb, vast ravines
Swell to the summer drone of fine machines.
The driver, melting down the distance here,
May cast in flight the faint hoof of a deer
Or pass the faint head set perplexedly.
And man-made stone outgrows the living tree,
And at its rising, air is shaken, men
Are shattered, and the tremor swells again,
Extending to the naked salty shore,
Rank with the sea, which crumbles evermore.

I now remembered slowly how I came,
I, sometime living, sometime with a name,
Creeping by iron ways across the bare
Wastes of Wyoming, turning in despair,
Changing and turning, till the fall of night,
Then throbbing motionless with iron might.
Four days and nights! Small stations by the way,
Sunk far past midnight! Nothing one can say
Names the compassion they stir in the heart.
Obscure men shift and cry, and we depart.

And I remembered with the early sun
That foul-mouthed barber back in Pendleton,
The sprawling streets, the icy station bench,
The Round-up pennants, the latrinal stench.
These towns are cold by day, the flesh of vice
Raw and decisive, and the will precise;
At night the turbulence of drink and mud,
Blue glare of gas, the dances dripping blood,
Fists thudding murder in the shadowy air,
Exhausted whores, sunk to a changeless stare.
Alive in empty fact alone, extreme,
They make each fact a mortuary dream.

Once when the train paused in an empty place,
I met the unmoved landscape face to face;
Smoothing abysses that no stream could slake,
Deep in its black gulch crept the heavy Snake,
The sound diffused, and so intently firm,
It seemed the silence, having change nor term.

Beyond the river, gray volcanic stone
In rolling hills: the river moved alone.
And when we started, charged with mass, and slow,
We hung against it in an awful flow.

Thus I proceeded until early night,
And, when I read the station's name aright,
Descended—at the bidding of a word!
I slept the night out where the thought occurred,
Then rose to view the dwelling where I lay.
Outside, the bare land stretching far away;
The frame house, new, fortuitous, and bright,
Pointing the presence of the morning light;
A train's far screaming, clean as shining steel
Planing the distance for the gliding heel.
Through shrinking frost, autumnal grass uncurled,
In naked sunlight, on a naked world.

Years had elapsed; the long room was the same.
At the far end, a log with drooping flame
Cast lengthening shadow. I was there alone,
A presence merely, like a shadow thrown,
Changing and growing dark with what I knew.
Above the roof, as if through a long flue,
The midnight wind poured steadily through pines.
I saw the trees flame thin, in watery lines.

Then, from my station in the empty air,
I saw them enter by the door; that pair
Opened and closed and watched each other move
With murderous eyes and gestures deep with love.
First came the Widow, but she had no face—
Naught but a shadow. At an earth-soaked pace
Her lover followed, weak with fear and lust.
And then I noticed there were years of dust
On floor and table, thought that in my day
No pines had been there. They sat down to play
At cards on a small table, and made tea,
And ate and played in silence. I could see
His lust come on him slowly, and his head
Fall on the table, but uncomforted
He feared to reach across to find her hand.
Deep in her veil I saw the features stand,
A deep jaw open; and a low iron laugh
Came from afar, a furious epigraph
To what I knew not in another place.
What evil was there in that woman's face!
He shrank in fear and told her of his love,
And she smiled coldly on him from above,

Stooped to a bundle lying by her side
And with a sodden tenderness untied
A severed head, gazed, and denied his plea.
He shuddered, heavy with lubricity.

There, steeped in the remote familiar gloom,
What were those demons doing in that room,
Their gestures aging, where the increasing shade
Stalked the dark flame that ever wearier played
As my receding memories left me dull?
My spirit now was but a shadowy hull.
Half-lost, I felt the Lover's shame my own.
I faced the Widow; we two were alone.

I saw the head and grasped it and struck root,
And then I rose, and with a steady foot,
I left her there, retarded in a dream.
Slowly I moved, like a directed beam.
My flesh fused with the cold flesh of the head;
My blood drew from me, from the neck flowed red,
A dark pulse on the darkness. The head stirred
Weakly beneath my fingers, and I heard
A whispered laughter, and the burden grew
In life and fury as my strength withdrew.
As if I labored up a flood of years,
I gathered heavy speed, drenched in arrears,
And limp to drowning, and I drove my flesh
Through the dark rooms adjacent to that mesh.
I was returning by the narrow hall;
Bound in my thought, jaw spread, I could not call.
And yet, with stride suspended in midair,
I fled more fast, yet more retarded there,
Swung backward by that laughter out of Hell,
Pealing at arm's length like an iron bell.

There in the darkest passage, where my feet
Fled fastest, he laughed loudest, and defeat
Was certain, for he held me in one place,
Fleeing immobile in an empty space,
I looked above me; on the stairway saw
The Widow, like a corpse. Fear drove my jaw
Wide open, and the tremor of that scream
Shattered my being like an empty dream.

Great eucalypti, black amid the flame,
Rise from below the slope, above his name.
The light is vibrant at their edges, clings,
Running in all ways through quick whisperings,
Falling in secrecy athwart each stone.
Under a little plaque he waits alone.
There is no faintest tremor in that urn.
Each flake of ash is sure in its return—
Never to alter, a pure quality,
A shadow cast against Eternity.

What has he found there? Life, it seems, is this:
To learn to shorten what has moved amiss;
To temper motion till a mean is hit,
Though the wild meaning would unbalance it;
To stand, precarious, near the utter end;
Betrayed, deserted, and alone descend,
Blackness before, and on the road above
The crowded terror that is human love;
To still the spirit till the flesh may lock
Its final cession in eternal rock.

Then let me pause in this symbolic air,
Each fiery grain immobile as despair,
Fixed at a rigid distance from the earth,
Absorbed each motion that arose from birth.
Here let me contemplate eternal peace,
Eternal station, which annuls release.
Here may I read its meaning, though the eye
Sear with the effort, ere the body die.
For what one is, one sees not; 'tis the lot
Of him at peace to contemplate it not.

ANACREONTIC

Peace! there is peace at last.
Deep in the Tuscan shade,
Swathed in the Grecian past,
Old Landor's bones are laid.

How many years have fled!
But o'er the sunken clay
Of the auguster dead
The centuries delay.

Come, write good verses, then!
That still, from age to age,
The eyes of able men
May settle on our page.

TO A YOUNG WRITER
Achilles Holt, Stanford, 1930

Here for a few short years
Strengthen affections; meet,
Later, the dull arrears
Of age, and be discreet.

The angry blood burns low.
Some friend of lesser mind
Discerns you not; but so
Your solitude's defined.

Write little; do it well.
Your knowledge will be such,
At last, as to dispel
What moves you overmuch.

TO MY INFANT DAUGHTER

I

Ah, could you now with thinking tongue
Discover what involvëd lies
In flesh and thought obscurely young,
What earth and age can worst devise!

Then I might thread my path across
Your sin and anguish; I might weigh
Minutely every gain and loss,
And time each motion of my day—

So break the impact of my wrath
To change some instant of your pain,
And clear the darkness from my path
That your decay were not in vain.

Whose hands will lay those hands to rest,
Those hands themselves, no more the same,
Will weeping lay them on the breast,
A token only and a name?

II

Alas, that I should be
So old, and you so small!
You will think naught of me
When your dire hours befall.

Take few men to your heart!
Unstable, fierce, unkind,
The ways that men impart.
True love is slow to find.

True art is slow to grow.
Like a belated friend,
It comes to let one know
Of what has had an end.

FOR MY FATHER'S GRAVE

Here lies one sweet of heart.
Stay! thou too must depart.
In silence set thy store—
These ashes speak no more.

The calloused grass lies hard
Against the cracking plain:
Life is a grayish stain;
The salt-marsh hems my yard.

Dry dikes rise hill on hill:
In sloughs of tidal slime
Shell-fish deposit lime,
Wild sea-fowl creep at will.

The highway, like a beach,
Turns whiter, shadowy, dry:
Loud, pale against the sky,
The bombing planes hold speech.

Yet fruit grows on the trees;
Here scholars pause to speak;
Through gardens bare and Greek,
I hear my neighbor's bees.

ELEGY ON A YOUNG AIREDALE BITCH
LOST SOME YEARS SINCE
IN THE SALT-MARSH

Low to the water's edge
You plunged; the tangled herb
Locked feet and mouth, a curb
Tough with the salty sedge.

Half dog and half a child,
Sprung from that roaming bitch,
You flung through dike and ditch,
Betrayed by what is wild.

The old dogs now are dead,
Tired with the hunt and cold,
Sunk in the earth and old.
But your bewildered head,

Led by what heron cry,
Lies by what tidal stream?—
Drenched with ancestral dream,
And cast ashore to dry.

Where he wandered, dream-enwound,
Brightness took the place of sound.
Shining plane and mass before:
Everywhere the sealèd door.
Children's unplacated grace
Met him with an empty face.
Mineral his limbs were grown:
Weight of being, not his own.
Ere he knew that he must die,
Ore had veinèd lip and eye:
Caught him scarcely looking back,
Startled at his golden track,
Immortalized the quickened shade
Of meaning by a moment made.

SONNET TO THE MOON

Now every leaf, though colorless, burns bright
With disembodied and celestial light,
And drops without a movement or a sound
A pillar of darkness to the shifting ground.

The lucent, thin, and alcoholic flame
Runs in the stubble with a nervous aim,
But, when the eye pursues, will point with fire
Each single stubble-tip and strain no higher.

O triple goddess! Contemplate my plight!
Opacity, my fate! Change, my delight!
The yellow tom-cat, sunk in shifting fur,
Changes and dreams, a phosphorescent blur.

Sullen I wait, but still the vision shun.
Bodiless thoughts and thoughtless bodies run.

THE ANNIVERSARY

To Achilles Holt

Where the summer stilled the vine,
We drank up a quart of wine.
Wine to parting! Man is free,
Half dissolved in memory.
Now the season is aflame,
Man has lost the way he came,
Turns confused. Momentum bends
Earth unto her fiery ends.
In the shining desert still
We must bend us to our will.
Crane is dead at sea. The year
Dwindles to a purer fear.

BEFORE DISASTER

Winter, 1932-3

Evening traffic homeward burns,
Swift and even on the turns,
Drifting weight in triple rows,
Fixed relation and repose.
This one edges out and by,
Inch by inch with steady eye.
But should error be increased,
Mass and moment are released;
Matter loosens, flooding blind,
Levels drivers to its kind.
   Ranks of nations thus descend,
Watchful to a stormy end.
By a moment's calm beguiled,
I have got a wife and child.
Fool and scoundrel guide the State.
Peace is whore to Greed and Hate.
Nowhere may I turn to flee:
Action is security.
Treading change with savage heel,
We must live or die by steel.

THE PRINCE

The prince or statesman who would rise to power
Must rise through shallow trickery, and speak
The tongue of knavery, deceive the hour,
Use the corrupt, and still corrupt the weak.

And he who having power would serve the State,
Must now deceive corruption unto good,
By indirection strengthen love with hate,
Must love mankind with craft and hardihood:

Betray the witless unto wisdom, trick
Disaster to good luck, escape the gaze
Of all the pure at heart, each lunatic
Of innocence, who draws you to his daze:

And this frail balance to immortalize,
Stare publicly from death through marble eyes.

PHASELLUS ILLE
After a poem by R. P. Blackmur

The dry wood strains, the small house stands its ground:
Jointed and tough, its sides shed off the storm.
And deep within, the heavy flame is warm,
Gold weight of peace on floor and chair enwound.
Wárm mínd, wárm héart, béam, bólt, and lóck,
You hold the love you took: and now, at length,
The mind and body, in new-wedded strength,
Toughen toward age, to brace against the shock.

Hold sure the course! the small house, like a boat,
Rides firm, intact, awaits the final blow.
Beneath, the current of impartial chance,
Disaster that strikes briefly and by rote,
The hazards of insane inheritance,
Láve our smóoth húll with what we little know.

ORPHEUS
In Memory of Hart Crane

Climbing from the Lethal dead,
Past the ruined waters' bed,
In the sleep his music cast
Tree and flesh and stone were fast—
As amid Dodona's wood
Wisdom never understood.

Till the shade his music won
Shuddered, by a pause undone—
Silence would not let her stay.
He could go one only way:
By the river, strong with grief,
Gave his flesh beyond belief.

Yet the fingers on the lyre
Spread like an avenging fire.
Crying loud, the immortal tongue,
From the empty body wrung,
Broken in a bloody dream,
Sang unmeaning down the stream.

A POST-CARD TO THE SOCIAL MUSE
WHO WAS INVOKED MORE FORMALLY
BY VARIOUS MARXIANS
AND OTHERS
IN THE PAGES
OF THE NEW REPUBLIC
DURING THE WINTER
OF 1932-3

Madam, since you choose
To call yourself a Muse,
   I will not be too nice
   To give advice.

Passion is hard of speech,
Wisdom exact of reach;
   Poets have studied verse;
   And wit is terse.

Change or repose is wrought
By steady arm and thought:
   The fine indignant sprawl
   Confuses all.

Do not engage with those
Of small verse and less prose;
   'Twere better far to play
   At bouts-rimés.

ON THE DEATH
OF SENATOR THOMAS J. WALSH

An old man more is gathered to the great.
 Singly, for conscience' sake he bent his brow:
He served that mathematic thing, the State,
 And with the great will be forgotten now.
The State is voiceless: only, we may write
 Singly our thanks for service past, and praise
The man whose purpose and remorseless sight
 Pursued corruption for its evil ways.

How sleep the great, the gentle, and the wise!
 Agëd and calm, they couch the wrinkled head.
Done with the wisdom that mankind devise,
 Humbly they render back the volume read—
Dwellers amid a peace that few surmise,
 Masters of quiet among all the dead.

DEDICATION FOR A BOOK OF CRITICISM

To W. D. Briggs

He who learns may feed on lies:
He who understands is wise.
He who understands the great
Joins them in their own estate:
Grasping what they had to give,
Adds his strength that they may live.

Strong the scholar is to scan
What is permanent in man;
To detect his form and kind
And preserve the human mind;
By the type himself to guide,
Universal wisdom bide.

Heir of Linacre and More,
Guardian of Erasmus' store,
Careful knower of the best,
Bacon's scholar, Jonson's guest,
It was in your speaking lip
That I honored scholarship.

In the motions of your thought
I a plan and model sought;
My deficiencies but gauge
My own talents and the age;
What is good from you I took:
Then, in justice, take my book.

A LEAVE-TAKING

I, who never kissed your head,
Lay these ashes in their bed;
That which I could do have done.
Now farewell, my newborn son.

ON TEACHING THE YOUNG

The young are quick of speech.
Grown middle-aged, I teach
Corrosion and distrust,
Exacting what I must.

A poem is what stands
When imperceptive hands,
Feeling, have gone astray.
It is what one should say.

Few minds will come to this.
The poet's only bliss
Is in cold certitude—
Laurel, archaic, rude.

CHIRON

I, who taught Achilles, saw
Leap beyond me by its law,
By intrinsic law destroyed,
Genius in itself alloyed.

Dying scholar, dim with fact,
By the stallion body racked,
Studying my long defeat,
I have mastered Jove's deceit.

Now my head is bald and dried,
Past division simplified:
On the edge of naught I wait,
Magnitude inviolate.

HERACLES

for Don Stanford

Eurystheus, trembling, called me to the throne,
Alcmena's son, heavy with thews and still.
He drove me on my fatal road alone:
I went, subservient to Hera's will.

For, when I had resisted, she had struck
Out of the sky and spun my wit: I slew
My children, quicker than a stroke of luck,
With motion lighter than my sinews knew.

Compelled down ways obscure with analogue
To force the Symbols of the Zodiac—
Bright Lion, Boundless Hydra, Fiery Dog—
I spread them on my arms as on a rack:

Spread them and broke them in the groaning wood,
And yet the Centaur stung me from afar,
His blood envenomed with the Hydra's blood:
Thence was I outcast from the earthy war.

Nessus the Centaur, with his wineskin full,
His branch and thyrsus, and his fleshy grip—
Her whom he could not force he yet could gull.
And she drank poison from his bearded lip.

Older than man, evil with age, is life:
Injustice, direst perfidy, my bane
Drove me to win my lover and my wife;
By love and justice I at last was slain.

The numbered Beings of the wheeling track
I carried singly to the empty throne,
And yet, when I had come exhausted back,
Was forced to wait without the gate alone.

Commanded thus to pause before the gate,
I felt from my hot breast the tremors pass,
White flame dissecting the corrupted State,
Eurystheus vibrant in his den of brass:

Vibrant with horror, though a jewelled king,
Lest, the heat mounting, madness turn my brain
For one dry moment, and the palace ring
With crystal terror ere I turn again.

This stayed me, too: my life was not my own,
But I my life's; a god I was, not man.
Grown Absolute, I slew my flesh and bone;
Timeless, I knew the Zodiac my span.

This was my grief, that out of grief I grew—
Translated as I was from earth at last,
From the sad pain that Deïanira knew.
Transmuted slowly in a fiery blast,

Perfect, and moving perfectly, I raid
Eternal silence to eternal ends:
And Deïanira, an imperfect shade,
Retreats in silence as my arc descends.

Now praise Alcmena for unchanging pride!
She sent her lover, when her brothers died,
To carry bloody death, where death was just;
The vengeance done, she yielded to his lust.
Zeus in the Theban halls her love besought:
To Zeus the greatest of his sons she brought:
The scion whom the god desired her for,
Alcides, Hero of Symbolic War.
She long outlived Alcides; when his son
Destroyed Eurystheus, and the feud was done,
She gouged the tyrant's eyes and cursed the head.
Then dense with age, she laid her on her bed.
But Zeus remembered the unbending dame,
Her giant maidenhood, the tireless frame,
That long had honored and had served him well,
And made her Rhadamanthus' queen in Hell.

THESEUS: A TRILOGY

for Henry Ramsey

I.   The Wrath of Artemis

On the wet sand the queen emerged from forest,
Tall as a man, half naked, and at ease,
Leaned on her bow and eyed them. This, the priestess,
Who, with her savages, had harried Greece
From south to east, and now fought down from Thrace,
Her arrows cold as moonlight, and her flesh
Bright as her arrows, and her hatred still.
Heracles eyed the ground, and Theseus watched her.
Remote and thin as a bird-call over ice
From deep in the forest came the cry of her warriors,
Defiance from Artemis, the evasive daemon:
Hippolyta smiled, but Heracles moved softly
And seized her suddenly, bore her to the ship,
Bound her and left her vibrating like a deer,
Astounded beyond terror. And her women
Fell as they came, like water to dry earth,
An inundation of the living moon.

From out the close hold of the nervous galley
She heard the shouting muffled in soft blood;
She heard it thinning quietly away.
And anger seized her; mind exceeded body,
Invoked divinity and rose to godhead:
She prayed the goddess to avenge the dead.
Then, in the doorway, blackened with maiden death,
Appeared the Attic conqueror in fulfillment.
Theseus, inexorable with love and war,
And ignorant with youth, begot upon her
A son, created in her shuddering fury,
To be born in Attica, the naked land.

In Attica, the naked land, she strode,
Brooding upon the secrets of the goddess,
Upon the wet bark of the Scythian forest,
The wet turf under bare foot, and the night
Blue with insistence of the staring eye.
The son, conceived in hatred, grew implacably,
Beyond her slow death, which he saw in passing,
Insolent, slender, effeminate, and chill,
His muscles made for running down the stag,
Dodging the boar, which Theseus would have broken,
Keeping step with the moon's shadows, changing
From thought to thought with an unchanging face.
He, judging Theseus from his narrow wisdom,
Yet judged him, and exiled him from his quiet,
The wrath of Artemis grown part of Theseus,
A man of moonlight and intensive calm.

II.   Theseus and Ariadne

After the mossy night and the wet stone,
The grappling with the wet hair of the beast,
After the slow and careful fingering
Of the pale linen on the cold return,
Theseus emerged. Ariadne awaited him,
Her face half hidden with black hair and shame.
And Theseus spoke:

     The Minotaur is dead.
Pasiphaë the white will sin no more:
The daughter of the moon, who bore this ghast
And dripping horror has been long at rest.
The sin of your blood I have extinguished; yet
Think not you will go quit. Your body is mine,
By all these tokens; and the taint of hell
Has eaten through my skin. Minos contrived
The trembling blackness of that hall of vision;
The prisoned fiend, your brother, beat me down,
I drew him after, and his blood burned through me,
Stinging more wildly than your body.

         She:
My mother's sin has poisoned you, and I
Was poisoned long ago. We share this crime,
And I am yours, I know not to what end.
Minos' vengeance is buried in our two bodies.
You had me from Minos, should you prevail,
And Minos is the will of Zeus, withdraws not.
I am motionless in the scales of Justice.
We go now to your ship; the carven wood
Will glide in quiet from the rocks of Crete,
That bloodstained island of the gods, and we
Shall set our feet in peace on lesser isles.

So Theseus took her by the hand, boarded
The limber galley, and the foam distended
Coldly above the crash on rock. The boat,
Quick on the heavy tumult, scoured the inlets
And found that island where he slew her, yet
Escaped not, took her sister, her for whom
Poseidon betrayed him, when he slew his son.

III. The Old Age of Theseus

He gathered Phaedra, hard with childhood, small,
Shivering in arm and breast, into his arms.
He knew his age at last. Sin with this child
Was sin in solitude. Arms that had bound
The Heraclean bull, Phaea the sow,
That had fought side by side with Heracles
And beat their black way from the ice of Lethe,
Were hard with realized identity,
Beyond her comprehension, and he lay
Whole in the salty toughness of his age.

When he set foot in Attica, he found
Aegeus at rest, and he assumed the State.
Here were abstractions fitter for his years:
The calculation of corruption, thus
To balance evil against evil surely
And establish immitigable good.

                        He ruled
Hard in his certitude through Phaedra's death,
The betrayal of his son, that eccentricity
Of furious children. And he gathered up
The knowledge of his youth: the steady shame
Of tall Hippolyta; the calm of Aethra;
The quiet evil of the grave Medea;
The image of Pirithoüs in Hell,
Caught in the moving flesh among the shades—
Passion immovable!—the Orphic music
That swelled the measure of the Argo's oars
To a golden stride coëval with the Sun—
Gathered them slowly up and fed upon them,

Distilled from them the honey of calm wisdom—
The face of Ariadne dead, himself
Suddenly translated to another time.

Alone, he and the State. The State, established,
Exiled him into Scyros. Lycomedes,
The strange face of a king, was all that stood
Between him and himself. And Lycomedes,
The treacherous host, betrayed him to the State,
Which had betrayed him, to which he had been betrayed
By every movement of his flesh and spirit;
So cast him from the rock to solitude,
To the cold perfection of unending peace.

SOCRATES

for Clayton Stafford

We come now to the hemlock: this, the test
Of my daimonic promptings, of my long
Uncertain labor to discern the best,
To formulate forever what is wrong.

What is the city? What historic crux
Have we aproached? Could but my skill endure,
The mind of Athens might surpass the flux,
When tongue and stone subside, her thought be sure.

If of my talking there should come a soul
Of tougher thought in richer phrase empearled,
Then were I sire and grandsire, scroll by scroll,
The vast foundation of a Western World.

While arguing amid the colonnades,
Tired in the noon-day by the badly taught,
Or resting, dubious, in the laurel shades,
I have impinged upon a firmer thought;

Have raised the Timeless up against the times;
The times, in turn, with this insensate cup,
Judge definition the most fierce of crimes;
The Timeless bids me drink the judgment up.

Thus are the times transmuted: understood,
A Timeless Form, comprising my estate.
Though what escapes them is my proper good,
Yet still would I be, so must they be, great.

Consistency gives quiet to the end.
My enemy is but a type of man,
And him whom I have changed, I call my friend.
The mind is formed. Dissuade it, he who can.

TO EDWIN V. McKENZIE
On his defense of David Lamson

The concept lives, but few men fill the frame;
Greatness is difficult: the certain aim,
The powerful body, and the nervous skill,
The acquiring mind, and the untiring will,
The just man's fury and uplifted arm,
And the strong heart, to keep the weak from harm.
This is the great man of tradition, one
To point out justice when the wrong is done;
To outwit rogue and craven; represent
Mankind in the eternal sacrament—
Odysseus, with the giant weapon bent.

When those who guard tradition in the schools
Proved to be weaklings and half-learnëd fools,
You took the burden, saved the intellect.
Combating treason, mastering each defect,
You fought your battle, inch by inch of ground.
When Justice had become an angry sound,
When Judgment dwindled to an angry man,
You named the limits of the civil span:
I saw you, mantled in tradition, tower;
You filled the courtroom with historic power;
Yourself the concept in the final hour.

TO A WOMAN ON HER DEFENSE OF HER BROTHER UNJUSTLY CONVICTED OF MURDER
Written after an initial study of the evidence

The villainy of pride in scholarship,
The villainy of cold impartial hate,
The brutal quiet of the lying lip,
The brutal power, judicial and sedate,

The calculation of the shifting friend,
The changing eye, the closed and narrowing scene,
The steady vision of the awful end,
Outrage and anarchy in formal mien;

These for an evil year now you have fought,
Which for three weeks, through nervous nights awake,
I learned could break me, for the Devil wrought.
May God support you, for your brother's sake!

There is a special Hell for each of these:
The brute, succumbing where his judgments err,
Compels the cringing fool to perjuries;
The friend begs comfort of the perjurer;

The scholar, now discovering his allies,
And turning to himself to stay his doom,
Finds but his pride amid a nest of lies,
A dire obsession in an empty room.

And what of him whom men at last disown!
Whom circumstance, guided by evil will,
Struck when his mind had broken! Locked in stone,
He waits the summons of the State to kill.

Ah, should you lose at last, yet you and he,
Each in the certitude the other gave,
Strong in your love, and by your love made free,
Would bear some goodness to the utter grave!

Yet may you two, bound in a stronger whole,
Firm in disaster, amid evil true,
Give us some knowledge of the human soul
And bend our spirits to the human due!

TO DAVID LAMSON
Awaiting retrial, in the jail at San José

If I ever pleased the Muse,
May she not one boon refuse;
May I ages hence rehearse
Darkest evil in my verse;
May I state my grief and shame
At the scholar's empty name:
How great scholars failed to see
Virtue in extremity;
How the special intellect
Fortified them in neglect,
Left their feelings, brutal, wild,
By inconsequence beguiled;
Wisdom brought to final rest,
Learning's very name a jest,
And the wise, like village fools,
County politicians' tools;
How I found a quiet friend,
Working at the evening's end,
Far beyond the tongues that rail,
Hidden in the county jail,
Who, unchanged amid disease,
Wrote with power and spoke with ease,
Who, though human thought decayed,
Yet the dissolution stayed,
Gracious in that evil shade.

JOHN DAY, FRONTIERSMAN

Among the first and farthest! Elk and deer
Fell as your rifle rang in rocky caves;
There your lean shadow swept the still frontier,
Your eyes regarded the Columbia's waves.

Amid the stony winter, gray with care,
Hunted by savages from sleep to sleep
—Those patriots of darkness and despair!—
You climbed in solitude what rigid steep!

Broken at last by very force of frame,
By wintry hunger like a warrior's brand,
You died a madman. And now bears your name
A gentle river in a fertile land.

The eminence is gone that met your eye;
The winding savage, too, has sunk away.
Now, like a summer myth, the meadows lie,
Deep in the calm of silvan slow decay.

I was the patriarch of the shining land,
Of the blond summer and metallic grain;
Men vanished at the motion of my hand,
And when I beckoned they would come again.

The earth grew dense with grain at my desire;
The shade was deepened at the springs and streams;
Moving in dust that clung like pillared fire,
The gathering herds grew heavy in my dreams.

Across the mountains, naked from the heights,
Down to the valley broken settlers came,
And in my houses feasted through the nights,
Rebuilt their sinews and assumed a name.

In my clear rivers my own men discerned
The motive for the ruin and the crime—
Gold heavier than earth, a wealth unearned,
Loot, for two decades, from the heart of Time.

Metal, intrinsic value, deep and dense,
Preanimate, inimitable, still,
Real, but an evil with no human sense,
Dispersed the mind to concentrate the will.

Grained by alchemic change, the human kind
Turned from themselves to rivers and to rocks;
With dynamite broke metal unrefined;
Measured their moods by geologic shocks.

With knives they dug the metal out of stone;
Turned rivers back, for gold through ages piled,
Drove knives to hearts, and faced the gold alone;
Valley and river ruined and reviled;

107

Reviled and ruined me, my servant slew,
Strangled him from the figtree by my door.
When they had done what fury bade them do,
I was a cursing beggar, stripped and sore.

What end impersonal, what breathless age,
Incontinent of quiet and of years,
What calm catastrophe will yet assuage
This final drouth of penitential tears?

Spreading and low, unwatered, concentrate
Of years of growth that thickens, not expands,
With leaves like mica and with roots that grate
Upon the deep foundations of these lands,
In your brown shadow, on your heavy loam
—Leaves shrinking to the whisper of decay—
What feet have come to roam,
                         what eyes to stay?
Your motion has o'ertaken what calm hands?

Quick as a sunbeam, when a bird divides
The lesser branches, on impassive ground,
Hwui-Shan, the ancient, for a moment glides,
Demure with wisdom, and without a sound;
Brown feet that come to meet him, quick and shy,
Move in the flesh, then, browner, dry to bone;
The brook-like shadows lie
                         where sun had shone;
Ceaseless, the dead leaves gather, mound on mound.

And where they gather, darkening the glade,
In hose and doublet, and with knotty beard,
Armed with the musket and the pirate's blade,
Stern as the silence by the savage feared,
Drake and his seamen pause to view the hills,
Measure the future with a steady gaze.
But when they go naught fills
                         the patient days;
The bay lies empty where the vessels cleared.

The Spaniard, learning caution from the trees,
Building his dwelling from the native clay,
Took native concubines: the blood of these
Calming his blood, he made a longer stay.
Longer, but yet recessive, for the change
Came on his sons and their sons to the end;
For peace may yet derange
                              and earth may bend
The ambitious mind to an archaic way.

Then the invasion! and the soil was turned,
The hidden waters drained, the valleys dried;
And whether fire or purer sunlight burned,
No matter! one by one the old oaks died.
Died or are dying! The archaic race—
Black oak, live oak, and valley oak—ere long
Must crumble on the place
                              which they made strong
And in the calm they guarded now abide.

ON REREADING A PASSAGE
FROM JOHN MUIR

Seeking in vain to find the heroic brow,
The subject fitting for a native ode,
I turn from thinking, for there haunts me now
A wrinkled figure on a dusty road:
Climbing from road to path, from path to rock,
From rock to live oak, thence to mountain bay,
Through unmoved twilight, where the rifle's shock
Was half absorbed by leaves and drawn away,
Through mountain lilac, where the brown deer lay.

This was my childhood's revery: to be
Not one who seeks in nature his release
But one forever by the dripping tree,
Paradisaïc in his pristine peace.
I might have been this man: a knowing eye
Moving on leaf and bark, a quiet gauge
Of growing timber and of climbing fly,
A quiet hand to fix them on the page—
A gentle figure from a simpler age.

Under the forest, where the day is dark
And air is motionless throughout the day,
Rooted in leaf-mould and in rotting bark,
This old arbutus gathers strength to stay.

Tall as a man, and taller, but more old,
This is no shrub of some few years, but hard
Its smooth unbending trunk, oh, hard and cold!
Of earth and age the stony proof and guard!

The skin is rose: yet infinitely thin,
It is a color only. What one tells
Of ancient wood and softly glinting skin
Is less than are the tiny waxen bells.

This life is not our life; nor for our wit
The sweetness of these shades; these are alone.
There is no wisdom here; seek not for it!
This is the shadow of the vast madrone.

Reptilian green the wrinkled throat,
Green as a bough of yew the beard;
He bent his head, and so I smote;
Then for a thought my vision cleared.

The head dropped clean; he rose and walked;
He fixed his fingers in the hair;
The head was unabashed and talked;
I understood what I must dare.

His flesh, cut down, arose and grew.
He bade me wait the season's round,
And then, when he had strength anew,
To meet him on his native ground.

The year declined; and in his keep
I passed in joy a thriving yule;
And whether waking or in sleep,
I lived in riot like a fool.

He beat the woods to bring me meat.
His lady, like a forest vine,
Grew in my arms; the growth was sweet;
And yet what thoughtless force was mine!

By practice and conviction formed,
With ancient stubbornness ingrained,
Although her body clung and swarmed,
My own identity remained.

Her beauty, lithe, unholy, pure,
Took shapes that I had never known;
And had I once been insecure,
Had grafted laurel in my bone.

And then, since I had kept the trust,
Had loved the lady, yet was true,
The knight withheld his giant thrust
And let me go with what I knew.

I left the green bark and the shade,
Where growth was rapid, thick, and still;
I found a road that men had made
And rested on a drying hill.

AN OCTOBER NOCTURNE
October 31st, 1936

The night was faint and sheer;
Immobile, road and dune.
Then, for a moment, clear,
A plane moved past the moon.

O spirit cool and frail,
Hung in the lunar fire!
Spun wire and brittle veil!
And trembling slowly higher!

Pure in each proven line!
The balance and the aim,
Half empty, half divine!
I saw how true you came.

Dissevered from your cause,
Your function was your goal.
Oblivious of my laws,
You made your calm patrol.

The little snake now grieves
With whispering pause, and slow,
Uncertain where to go
Among the glassy leaves,
Pale angel that deceives.

With tongue too finely drawn,
Too pure, too tentative,
He needs but move to live,
Yet where he was is gone;
He loves the quiet lawn.

Kin to the petal, cool,
Translucent, veinëd, firm,
The fundamental worm,
The undefinëd fool,
Dips to the icy pool.

Amid the iris and the rose,
The honeysuckle and the bay,
The wild earth for a moment goes
In dust or weed another way.

Small though its corner be, the weed
Will yet intrude its creeping beard;
The harsh blade and the hairy seed
Recall the brutal earth we feared.

And if no water touch the dust
In some far corner, and one dare
To breathe upon it, one may trust
The spectre on the summer air:

The risen dust alive with fire,
The fire made visible, a blur
Interrate, the pervasive ire
Of foxtail and of hoarhound burr.

THE CREMATION
E. H. L.: 1866 - 1938

In Egypt, these five thousand years,
Men char with time, yet undispersed.
But we, whose mortal vision clears,
In one compact and final crash
In which a lifetime is reversed,
Sever the body from its ash.

The ash is but a little dust,
The body is eternal light.
And where is that which made you just?
Which gathered light about the bone
And moved the tongue, in earth's despite?
The powdered lime sinks back alone.

Thus you have left a fainter trace
Of what the spirit bore for hire
—No bony outline of a face!—
Than ages of the drying dead.
Once and for all you went through fire:
There is no footprint where you tread.

AN ELEGY
for the U.S.N. Dirigible, Macon

The noon is beautiful: the perfect wheel
Now glides on perfect surface with a sound
Earth has not heard before; the polished ground
Trembles and whispers under rushing steel.

The polished ground, and prehistoric air!
Metal now plummets upward and there sways,
A loosened pendulum for summer days,
Fixing the eyeball in a limpid stare.

There was one symbol in especial, one
Great form of thoughtless beauty that arose
Above the mountains, to foretell the close
Of this deception, at meridian.

Steel-gray the shadow, than a storm more vast!
Its crowding engines, rapid, disciplined,
Shook the great valley like a rising wind.
This image, now, is conjured from the past.

Wind in the wind! O form more light than cloud!
Storm amid storms! And by the storms dispersed!
The brain-drawn metal rose until accursed
By its extension and the sky was loud!

Who will believe this thing in time to come?
I was a witness. I beheld the age
That seized upon a planet's heritage
Of steel and oil, the mind's viaticum:

Crowded the world with strong ingenious things,
Used the provision it could not replace,
To leave but Cretan myths, a sandy trace
Through the last stone age, for the pastoral kings.

The spring has darkened with activity.
The future gathers in vine, bush, and tree:
Persimmon, walnut, loquat, fig, and grape,
Degrees and kinds of color, taste, and shape.
These will advance in their due series, space
The season like a tranquil dwelling-place.
And yet excitement swells me, vein by vein:
I long to crowd the little garden, gain
Its sweetness in my hand and crush it small
And taste it in a moment, time and all!
These trees, whose slow growth measures off my years,
I would expand to greatness. No one hears,
And I am still retarded in duress!
And this is like that other restlessness
To seize the greatness not yet fairly earned,
One which the tougher poets have discerned—
Gascoigne, Ben Jonson, Greville, Raleigh, Donne,
Poets who wrote great poems, one by one,
And spaced by many years, each line an act
Through which few labor, which no men retract.
This passion is the scholar's heritage,
The imposition of a busy age,
The passion to condense from book to book
Unbroken wisdom in a single look,
Though we know well that when this fix the head,
The mind's immortal, but the man is dead.

TO A PORTRAIT OF MELVILLE
IN MY LIBRARY

O face reserved, unmoved by praise or scorn!
O dreadful heart that won Socratic peace!
What was the purchase-price of thy release?
What life was buried, ere thou rose reborn?
Rest here in quiet, now. Our strength is shorn.
Honor my books! Preserve this room from wrack!
Plato and Aristotle at thy back,
Above thy head this ancient powder-horn.

The lids droop coldly, and the face is still:
Wisdom and wilderness are here at poise,
Ocean and forest are the mind's device,
But still I feel the presence of thy will:
The midnight trembles when I hear thy voice,
The noon's immobile when I meet thine eyes.

A PRAYER FOR MY SON
*"Tangled with earth all ways
we move."* —*Janet Lewis*

Eternal Spirit, you
Whose will maintains the world,
Who thought and made it true;
The honey-suckle curled
Through the arbutus limb,
The leaves that move in air,
Are half akin to him
Whose conscious moving stare
Is drawn, yet stirs by will;
Whose little fingers bend,
Unbend, and then are still,
While the mind seeks an end.
At moments, like a vine,
He clambers through small boughs;
Then poised and half divine,
He waits with lifted brows.
To steep the mind in sense,
Yet never lose the aim,
Will make the world grow dense,
Yet by this way we came.
Earth and mind are not one,
But they are so entwined,
That this, my little son,
May yet one day go blind.
Eternal Spirit, you
Who guided Socrates,
Pity this small and new
Bright soul on hands and knees.

Amid these clear and windy hills
Heat gathers quickly and is gone;
Dust rises, moves, and briefly stills;
Our thought can scarcely pause thereon.

With pale bright leaf and shadowy stem,
Pellucid amid nervous dust,
By pre-Socratic stratagem,
Yet sagging with its weight of must,

The vineyard spreads beside the road
In repetition, point and line.
I sing, in this dry bright abode,
The praises of the native wine.

It yields the pleasure of the eye,
It charms the skin, it warms the heart;
When nights are cold and thoughts crowd high,
Then 'tis the solvent for our art.

When worn for sleep the head is dull,
When art has failed us, far behind,
Its sweet corruption fills the skull
Till we are happy to be blind.

So may I yet, as poets use,
My time being spent, and more to pay,
In this quick warmth the will diffuse,
In sunlight vanish quite away.

When I was young, with sharper sense,
The farthest insect cry I heard
Could stay me; through the trees, intense,
I watched the hunter and the bird.

Where is the meaning that I found?
Or was it but a state of mind,
Some old penumbra of the ground,
In which to be but not to find?

Now summer grasses, brown with heat,
Have crowded sweetness through the air;
The very roadside dust is sweet;
Even the unshadowed earth is fair.

The soft voice of the nesting dove,
And the dove in soft erratic flight
Like a rapid hand within a glove,
Caress the silence and the light.

Amid the rubble, the fallen fruit,
Fermenting in its rich decay,
Smears brandy on the trampling boot
And sends it sweeter on its way.

ON THE PORTRAIT OF A SCHOLAR
OF THE ITALIAN RENAISSANCE

The color, quick in fluid oil,
Affirms the flesh and lambent hair;
And darkness, in its fine recoil,
Confesses that the mind is there.

With heavy lip, with massive curls,
With wisdom weighted, strong and dense,
The flesh is luminous as pearls;
The eyes ingenuous but intense.

The face is noble; but the name
Is one that we shall scarcely hold.
This is a vision in a frame,
Defined and matted down with gold.

Our names, with his, are but the lees
Residual from this clear intent;
Our finely grained identities
Are but this golden sediment.

A DEDICATION IN POSTSCRIPT
for my poems of 1940
Written to Agnes Lee shortly before her death

Because you labored still for Gautier's strength
In days when art was lost in breadth and length;
Because your friendship was a valued gift;
I send these poems—now, my only shift.
In the last years of your declining age,
I face again your cold immortal page:
The statue, pure amid the rotting leaves,
And her, forsaken, whom Truth undeceives.
Truth is the subject, and the hand is sure.
The hand once lay in mine: this will endure
Till all the casual errors fall away.
And art endures, or so the masters say.

A WINTER EVENING
near Alviso, California

The earth for miles is massed with wet:
Small tree and bush and hedge of briar
Have sunk from shape with help nor let
As rank confusion gathers higher.

Each little house beside the road,
In weedy field, with rotting fence,
Groans and subsides, a broken load
Dropped there by thwarted diligence.

And by a swollen ditch, a dog,
Mud-soaked and happy, in a daze
Works into rain as dark as fog,
And moves down coldly solvent ways.

With visionary care
The mind imagines Hell,
Draws fine the sound of flame
Till one can scarcely tell
The nature, or the name,
Or what the thing is for:

Past summer bough and cry,
The sky, distended, bare,
Now whispers like a shell
Of the increase of war.

Thus will man reach an end:
In fear of his own will,
Yet moved where it may tend,
With mind and word grown still.

The fieldmouse and the hare,
The small snake of the garden,
Whose little muscles harden,
Whose eyes now quickened stare,
Though driven by the sound
—Too small and free to pardon!—
Will repossess this ground.

A TESTAMENT

to one now a child

We will and move: the gain
Is purchased with our pain;
   The very strength we choose
    With what we lose.

God is revealed in this:
That some go not amiss,
   But through hard labor teach
    What we may reach.

These gave us life through death:
Jesus of Nazareth,
   Archaic Socrates,
    And such as these.

O small and fair of face!
In this appalling place,
   The conscious soul must give
    Its life to live.

TO A MILITARY RIFLE
1942

The times come round again;
The private life is small;
And individual men
Are counted not at all.
Now life is general,
And the bewildered Muse,
Thinking what she has done,
Confronts the daily news.

Blunt emblem, you have won:
With carven stock unbroke,
With core of steel, with crash
Of mass, and fading smoke;
Your fire leaves little ash;
Your balance on the arm
Points whither you intend;
Your bolt is smooth with charm.
When other concepts end,
This concept, hard and pure,
Shapes every mind therefor.
The time is yours, be sure,
Old Hammerheel of War.

I cannot write your praise
When young men go to die;
Nor yet regret the ways
That ended with this hour.
The hour has come. And I,
Who alter nothing, pray
That men, surviving you,
May learn to do and say
The difficult and true,
True shape of death and power.

FOR THE OPENING OF THE
WILLIAM DINSMORE BRIGGS ROOM *
Stanford University, May 7, 1942

Because our Being grows in mind,
And evil in imperfect thought,
And passion running undefined
May ruin what the masters taught;

Within the edge of war we meet
To dedicate this room to one
Who made his wisdom more complete
Than any save the great have done.

That in this room, men yet may reach,
By labor and wit's sullen shock,
The final certitude of speech
Which Hell itself cannot unlock.

* A reading room for graduate students in English, established as a memorial to the late head of the Stanford English department.

MOONLIGHT ALERT
Los Altos, California, June 1943

The sirens, rising, woke me; and the night
Lay cold and windless; and the moon was bright,
Moonlight from sky to earth, untaught, unclaimed,
An icy nightmare of the brute unnamed.
This was hallucination. Scarlet flower
And yellow fruit hung colorless. That hour
No scent lay on the air. The siren scream
Took on the fixity of shallow dream.
In the dread sweetness I could see the fall,
Like petals sifting from a quiet wall,
Of yellow soldiers through indifferent air,
Falling to die in solitude. With care
I held this vision, thinking of young men
Whom I had known and should not see again,
Fixed in reality, as I in thought.
And I stood waiting, and encountered naught.

The nervous light above my door
Towers high with blossoms; all their scent
Is shaken with the climbing roar
Of planes which thread the firmament.

Young men, preoccupied, alone,
Learn to control the earth and air;
Yet what is mine should be their own
And interpenetrate their care:

The perils of immortal mind,
The core of empire in a word,
The worth of states grown hard to find
Because true meaning is unheard;

The deviation from the strength
Which forms our motion, and the phrase
Which cheapens thought and yet at length
Would simulate more honest ways;

This fine deceit, this perfect rift,
Dissociating thought from sense,
I traced in quiet; and the shrift
Of wrath was all my recompense.

NIGHT OF BATTLE

Europe: 1944
as regarded from a great distance

Impersonal the aim
Where giant movements tend;
Each man appears the same;
Friend vanishes from friend.

In the long path of lead
That changes place like light
No shape of hand or head
Means anything tonight.

Only the common will
For which explosion spoke;
And stiff on field and hill
The dark blood of the folk.

AN ODE
ON THE DESPOILERS
OF LEARNING
IN AN AMERICAN UNIVERSITY
1947

This was our heritage:
In Learning's monument
To study, and teach the young,
Until our days were spent;
To reëmbody mind
In age succeeding age,
That some few men might see,
Though, mostly, men were blind;
To hold what men had wrung
From struggle to atone
For man's stupidity,
In labor and alone.

But now the insensate, calm
Performers of the hour,
Cold, with cold eye and palm,
Desiring trivial power,
And terror-struck within
At their own emptiness,
Move in. As they move in,
Slow and invidious,
They pause and calculate,
Then, as such beings use,
With long-perfected hate,
Strike the immortal Muse.

What art of prose or verse
Should bring their like to book?
What consecrated curse
And pious rhetoric?
Not one: we need but look.
For these have come too far:
They stand here, coarse and lined,
And permanent as stone,
In the final light of mind.
The body politic
Of Learning is its own
Inscrutable old Bar.

TO HERMAN MELVILLE IN 1951

Saint Herman, grant me this: that I may be
Saved from the worms who have infested thee.

TO THE HOLY SPIRIT

*from a deserted graveyard
in the Salinas Valley*

Immeasurable haze:
The desert valley spreads
Up golden river-beds
As if in other days.
Trees rise and thin away,
And past the trees, the hills,
Pure line and shade of dust,
Bear witness to our wills:
We see them, for we must;
Calm in deceit, they stay.

High noon returns the mind
Upon its local fact:
Dry grass and sand; we find
No vision to distract.
Low in the summer heat,
Naming old graves, are stones
Pushed here and there, the seat
Of nothing, and the bones
Beneath are similar:
Relics of lonely men,
Brutal and aimless, then,
As now, irregular.

These are thy fallen sons,
Thou whom I try to reach.
Thou whom the quick eye shuns,
Thou dost elude my speech.
Yet when I go from sense
And trace thee down in thought,
I meet thee, then, intense,
And know thee as I ought.
But thou art mind alone,
And I, alas, am bound
Pure mind to flesh and bone,
And flesh and bone to ground.

These had no thought: at most
Dark faith and blinding earth.
Where is the trammeled ghost?
Was there another birth?
Only one certainty
Beside thine unfleshed eye,
Beside the spectral tree,
Can I discern: these die.
All of this stir of age,
Though it elude my sense
Into what heritage
I know not, seems to fall,
Quiet beyond recall,
Into irrelevance.

A FRAGMENT

I cannot find my way to Nazareth.
I have had enough of this. Thy will is death,
And this unholy quiet is thy peace.
Thy will be done; and let discussion cease.

A SONG IN PASSING

Where am I now? And what
Am I to say portends?
Death is but death, and not
The most obtuse of ends.

No matter how one leans
One yet fears not to know.
God knows what all this means!
The mortal mind is slow.

Eternity is here.
There is no other place.
The only thing I fear
Is the Almighty Face.

TO THE MOON

Goddess of poetry,
Maiden of icy stone
With no anatomy,
Between us two alone
Your light falls thin and sure
On all that I propound.

Your service I have found
To be no sinecure;
For I must still inure
My words to what I find,
Though it should leave me blind
Ere I discover how.

What brings me here? Old age.
Here is the written page.
What is your pleasure now?

AT THE SAN FRANCISCO AIRPORT

To my daughter, 1954

This is the terminal: the light
Gives perfect vision, false and hard;
The metal glitters, deep and bright.
Great planes are waiting in the yard—
They are already in the night.

And you are here beside me, small,
Contained and fragile, and intent
On things that I but half recall—
Yet going whither you are bent.
I am the past, and that is all.

But you and I in part are one:
The frightened brain, the nervous will,
The knowledge of what must be done,
The passion to acquire the skill
To face that which you dare not shun.

The rain of matter upon sense
Destroys me momently. The score:
There comes what will come. The expense
Is what one thought, and something more—
One's being and intelligence.

This is the terminal, the break.
Beyond this point, on lines of air,
You take the way that you must take;
And I remain in light and stare—
In light, and nothing else, awake.

TWO OLD-FASHIONED SONGS

I. *Danse Macabre*

Who was who and where were they
Scholars all and bound to go
Iambs without heel or toe
Something one would never say
Moving in a certain way

Students with an empty book
Poets neither here nor there
Critics without face or hair
Something had them on the hook
Here was neither king nor rook

This is something some one said
I was wrong and he was right
Indirection in the night
Every second move was dead
Though I came I went instead

II. *A Dream Vision*

What was all the talk about?
This was something to decide.
It was not that I had died.
Though my plans were new, no doubt,
There was nothing to deride.

I had grown away from youth,
Shedding error where I could;
I was now essential wood,
Concentrating into truth;
What I did was small but good.

Orchard tree beside the road,
Bare to core, but living still!
Moving little was my skill.
I could hear the farting toad
Shifting to observe the kill,

Spotted sparrow, spawn of dung,
Mumbling on a horse's turd,
Bullfinch, wren, or mockingbird
Screaming with a pointed tongue
Objurgation without word.

The title *Collected Poems* may seem too ambitious for this volume; for the volume is not a complete collection of what I have published by a very wide margin. However, the volume contains everything which I wish to keep and represents in addition a kind of definition by example of the style which I have been trying to achieve for a matter of thirty years. The poems omitted seem to me inferior in quality, and they would certainly obscure the issue which for me is the principal issue.

For the reader who may not be familiar with some of the reference works which have beguiled my own leisure, I offer the following clarifications:

The Castle of Thorns. In medieval romance, which is for the most part a refurbishing of ancient folklore, the Robber Knight commonly represents Death. In taking his victim to his castle, which is normally surrounded by a wood of thorn, he must in some way cross or dive under water, which is the most ancient symbol of the barrier between the two worlds.

The Invaders are the modern physical scientists, of whom I would not write in quite the same terms today.

Heracles is treated as a Sun-god, the particular statement used being that of Anthon's *Classical Dictionary.* Allegorically, he is the artist, in hand-to-hand or semi-intuitive combat with experience.

The California Oaks. There is a brief account of Hwui-Shan on pages 24-5 of *A History of California; the Spanish Period,* by Charles Edward Chapman. Hwui-Shan was a Chinese Buddhist priest, who may have come to California in 499 A.D. According to Chapman, the story is found in Volume 231 of the great Chinese Encyclopedia and is found in other works and has long been known to Chinese scholars. Chapman believes that there were other Chinese voyages to the west coast of North America at very early dates.